The Answers Book for Kids

Volume 2

22 Questions on Dinosaurs and the Flood of Noah

Master Books®
P.O. Box 726
Green Forest, AR 72638

Master Books® is a division of the New Leaf Publishing Group, Inc.

Printed in China

Cover Design by Rebekah Krall
Interior Design by Terry White

ISBN 13: 978-0-89051-527-3
Library of Congress number: 2008929454

All Scripture references are New King James Version unless otherwise noted.

Please visit our website for other great titles: www.masterbooks.net

When you see this icon, there will be related Scripture references
noted for parents to use in answering their children's, and even their
own, questions.

For Parents and Teachers

Look now at the behemoth, which I made along with you; he eats grass like an ox.
See now, his strength is in his hips, and his power is in his stomach muscles.
He moves his tail like a cedar; the sinews of his thighs are tightly knit.
His bones are like beams of bronze, his ribs like bars of iron (Job 41:15–18).

Dear Moms and Dads:

As I have traveled the world these past 30+ years, I realize that dinosaurs are used more than almost anything else to indoctrinate children (and teens and adults) into believing the idea of millions of years of earth history.

Many Christian parents have been unable to counter this indoctrination because they don't know how to answer questions about dinosaurs, the fossil record, and the age of the earth. They cannot defend biblical authority and the Genesis history that is foundational to the rest of the Bible.

Sadly, when children don't get biblical answers, many of them are put on a slippery slide to unbelief — doubting the first part of the Bible (Genesis). This can ultimately lead to their doubt and unbelief of the rest of the Bible.

As parents, we are admonished to make known to our children the wonderful works of God — *"that the generation to come might know them, the children who would be born, that they may arise and declare them to their children, that they may set their hope in God, and not forget the works of God"* (Psalm 78:6–7). What an awesome privilege and responsibility God has given us!

My prayer is that this book will give crucial answers to assist you in building within your children a foundation to know and trust God's Word — right from the very first verse — and that one day they may put their faith in our Savior — the Creator of the universe — Jesus Christ.

Ken Ham
President/CEO, Answers in Genesis

Question: Were people different before the Flood than they are today?

Olivia K.

Age 11 — Australia

Answer:

Now the whole earth had one language and one speech. . . . "Come, let Us go down and there confuse their language, that they may not understand one another's speech" (Genesis 11:1, 7).

All people are of one race (descended from Adam), created in the image of God. But Olivia, I'm sure you see unique differences in people, even in your neighborhood. The Bible tells us what happened between Noah and today that caused such differences in people to arise. After the Flood, the people became prideful in their own efforts and disobeyed God's command to spread out over the earth. They built the Tower of Babel to worship the heavens instead of worshiping God.

So God confused their language — resulting in different language groups being formed. They could no longer understand one another. This caused them to move away from each other. And as the various groups became more and more separated, minor differences in groups arose as a result of the differing combinations of human genes. So, yes, I believe the people were probably a bit different back before the Flood because they spoke the same language and looked more similar than humans do today — but we are still humans belonging to one race.

Genesis 11:1–9

HOLY BIBLE

Question: Did Noah take dinosaurs on the ark?

Joy B.

Age 10 — Michigan, USA

6

Answer:

And of every living thing of all flesh you shall bring two of every sort into the ark, to keep them alive with you; they shall be male and female (Genesis 6:19).

Can you even imagine it? Dinosaurs on the ark? It is so very cool to think about. And we can be *sure* they were there because the Bible tells us that every kind of air-breathing, land-dwelling animal went aboard. Now, Noah did not know of the word dinosaur back then. In fact, that word was made up in 1841 to describe land animals found that had very unique bone structures, uncommon to other animals. Dinosaur literally means "Terrible Lizard."

But we do know what God tells us — that *all* the kinds of land animals were on the ark. Well, that just *had* to include the dinosaur kinds, too!

Genesis 6:19–20, 7:14

Question: How did all the dinosaurs fit on the ark?

Abby G.

Age 6 — New Mexico, USA

8

Answer:

And this is how you shall make it: The length of the ark shall be three hundred cubits, its width fifty cubits, and its height thirty cubits (Genesis 6:15).

Abby, your question is often asked by people a lot older than six! First of all, God told Noah how big to make the ark (see our verse). You might ask, what is a cubit? I believe the cubit that was used was about 20 inches long . . . and that would make the ark as long as one and a half football fields — about 510 feet (155 meters) — as tall as a 4-story building — about 45 feet (14 meters) — and about 85 feet (23 meters) wide! It was really big! Now another thing is that although there are hundreds of names of dinosaurs, there were probably only about 50 actual kinds. So, there may have only been a total of 100 dinosaurs on the ark. That still seems like a lot, doesn't it?

But, did you know that most dinosaurs were actually quite small? In fact, the average size of a dinosaur is the size of a sheep. (Some were as small as chickens!) And for the few dinosaurs that grew large, it would make sense that God would send smaller young adults. You know, after looking at all of these facts, I think there was plenty of room on the ark for the dinosaurs and all the other animals God sent to survive the Flood.

Genesis 1:25, 7:14

HOLY BIBLE

9

Question:

How did Noah get two of every sea animal on the ark?

Heidi C.

Age 10 — Ohio, USA

10

Answer:

Of the birds after their kind, of animals after their kind, and of every creeping thing of the earth after its kind, two of every kind will come to you to keep them alive (Genesis 6:20).

So, did Noah need a great big aquarium on board the ark? No, not at all! See our Bible verse, Heidi? It doesn't mention sea animals, does it? Noah didn't need to build an aquarium because the ark was sailing in one . . . and it was plenty big!

We know that many sea animals were killed in the Flood because most of the fossils we have are of sea creatures. The Flood was hard on them because the water was rough, the mud and sediment buried them, and the water temperatures and amount of salt were changing. But God allowed enough of them to survive the Flood so that we still have all the sea creature kinds we see today.

Genesis 6:17, 7:15, 7:22

Question:

Did Noah have to estimate how much food to gather or did God tell him?

Heidi C.

Age 10 — Ohio, USA

12

Answer:

And you shall take for yourself of all food that is eaten, and you shall gather it to yourself; and it shall be food for you and for them (Genesis 6:21).

Often we wish the Bible would give us more details, don't we? But, we know from our verse that God said to take food on board. It could be that God told Noah exactly what to take, but it just wasn't written down. It is also possible that Noah, who was almost 500 years old when God told him about the Flood, knew a lot about animals, like what and how much they needed to eat. Noah was, after all, very intelligent — smart enough to build the ark.

The animals couldn't have been as active while they were on the ark. You know, no more running, playing, swimming, chasing each other (they were on a boat, after all). So, I'm thinking they wouldn't have needed as much food to stay healthy and keep their bodies functioning properly. Again, we don't know what Noah did for sure, but I'm confident that Noah knew exactly what to bring and exactly how much to bring.

Genesis 7:5, 8:1

Question: How did Noah keep the animals on the ark from eating each other and his family?

Chase P.

Answer:

Then God remembered Noah, and every living thing, and all the animals that were with him in the ark. And God made a wind to pass over the earth, and the waters subsided (Genesis 8:1).

Our Bible verse tells us that God remembered Noah. God promised to deliver Noah and his family through the Flood. God was looking after Noah, and God was in control of every detail of Noah's voyage.

One possible answer to your question is that God could have miraculously stopped animals from eating each other. There is another possibility. We know that before sin, animals only ate vegetation. By the time of the Flood, a number of animals may have become vicious because of the effects of sin. But we notice today that even with animals like wolves — which are of the dog kind — there are other dogs that are not vicious. So God could have chosen the more friendly ones to represent a kind. God could also have supernaturally caused the animals to hibernate much of the time. And Noah no doubt built cages or rooms with doors to keep the animals from roaming the ark and possibly hurting other animals.

It is good to think about these things — it helps us to see there are many possible answers to your question.

But we can be sure that as God brought the different kinds of animals to Noah, He knew what was in store. He sent the animals to the ark and He would see that the animals and the people would survive the long trip together.

Genesis 1:29–30, 9:3

15

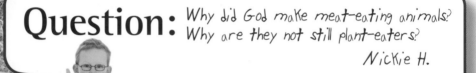

Question: Why did God make meat-eating animals? Why are they not still plant-eaters?

Nickie H.

Age 7 — Florida, USA

16

Answer:

Also, to every beast of the earth, to every bird of the air, and to everything that creeps on the earth, in which there is life, I have given every green herb for food (Genesis 1:30).

Once again, we can look to the Bible to give us the answer to our questions, Nickie. Originally, God did not create any meat-eating animals. All the animals were vegetarian, just like our Bible verse says. They were given every green herb (plants, grass, fruits, vegetables) for food. Now, eating all of those plants and vegetables and fruit might not be so easy without a good, sharp knife. And I believe that is why some animals have big, pointed, scary-looking teeth (well, scary in a fallen world)! After all, even some animals with sharp teeth today don't necessarily eat only meat. For instance, the panda has very sharp teeth and yet for the most part it still pretty much eats bamboo plants.

Because of sin, violence and death came into the world. Now, many animals eat other animals. But the Bible tells us that one day Jesus will restore His creation to its perfect state. There will no longer be sickness or death, and animals won't eat each other. What a glorious day that will be!

Genesis 6:13; Romans 6:23; Revelation 21:1–4

Question: Why did God allow some creatures to go extinct?

Ben D.

Age 10 — Canada

Answer:

. . . but of the tree of the knowledge of good and evil you shall not eat, for in the day that you eat of it you shall surely die (Genesis 2:17).

Ben, we know that some animals are extinct and some are on the endangered list, meaning they may soon become extinct. We need to understand that it is not God's fault the animals are going extinct. It's actually our fault because we sinned against God. When God first created the universe, He said it was all "very good." It was a place with no death or suffering anywhere! But Adam and Eve's disobedience to God brought death into the world — and the whole universe began to change because of God's judgment on our sin.

This was a very sad day because the very good universe now began to run down. Sin changed everything. With it came death, sickness, and suffering. Changes occurred in the weather, the food supply, the behavior of people, and the behavior of animals. These (and other) changes have contributed to why many animals have gone extinct.

But remember the good news! God promises to one day restore everything back to a perfect world where animals will no longer go extinct and people will no longer sin against God's commands.

Genesis 1:31; Romans 5:12; Psalm 33:20–22

Question: What happened to the ark once Noah, his family, and the animals got off?

Cameron P.

Age 10— South Carolina, USA

Answer:

Then God spoke to Noah, saying, "Go out of the ark, you and your wife, and your sons and your sons' wives with you" (Genesis 8:15–16).

The Flood destroyed everything on earth. Noah and his family remained in the ark while waiting for the waters to subside and the ground to dry out. But we know that they eventually left the ark. (I like to think about what a relief it must have been for them to breathe the fresh air and stand on solid ground again!)

The Bible mentions that Noah lived in a tent. It is very possible that Noah brought tents on the ark so he and his family would have places to live once the Flood was over. With everything else destroyed, and as Noah's family grew, the ark may have provided building materials for the homes and other buildings they would all eventually need. It may have decayed, been used as firewood, or destroyed by other means. If the ark did survive (and there is no real evidence it has) — the wood would have to be preserved in some way, like being petrified.

This is one of those things, Cameron, the Bible doesn't clearly tell us.

Genesis 8:4–16

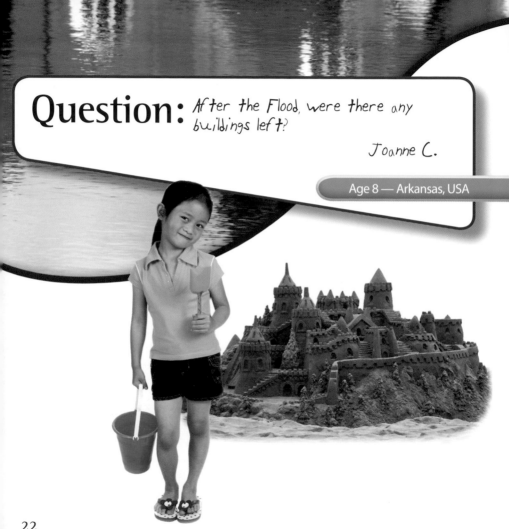

Question: After the Flood, were there any buildings left?

Joanne C.

Age 8 — Arkansas, USA

Answer:

So the LORD said, "I will destroy man whom I have created from the face of the earth, both man and beast, creeping thing and birds of the air . . . " (Genesis 6:7).

For the answer to this question, we're going to get a little lesson in geology (the study of rocks, canyons, and mountains). If you visit the Grand Canyon, there is what we call "basement" rocks that are a mile down into the canyon. These rocks are amazing in that it looks as though someone took a really sharp knife and just sliced the earth right off. On top of that you see layers of rocks, sand, and mud that were laid down by water right over the "basement" rocks. This gives some understanding of how devastating the Flood really was. How it just wiped out the surface of the earth. The Flood was cataclysmic — it was dreadful, tragic, a disaster, devastating. It destroyed everything and everyone on earth just as it was intended to do. So there wouldn't have been any buildings left from before the Flood.

Genesis 7:4; Luke 17:27

Question:

Did we use dinosaurs for transportation?

Joy B.

Age 10 — Michigan, USA

24

Answer:

For every kind of beast and bird, of reptile and creature of the sea, is tamed and has been tamed by mankind (James 3:7).

I know the Bible doesn't specifically address this question, but Joy, we can use the reasoning skills God gave us and His Word to come up with an answer. We see and hear about all sorts of animals being tamed by man. In fact, from our Bible verse it appears that we shouldn't be surprised that animals can be tamed. I can think of many animals that have been tamed to work for humans. There are elephants, tigers, bears, horses, dogs (of course), lions, camels, birds, dolphins, walruses, even the great killer whale, and a lot more! This is one of those things that is just fun to think about, isn't it? So, why not some of the dinosaurs? Who knows what they were doing? It seems to me we should at least allow the possibility that some could have been tamed to help with transportation, maybe even farming, hauling heavy loads (the strong ones!), and other things. After all, some dragon legends from China tell us that dragons (dinosaurs?) were used to pull the emperor's chariots.

Genesis 2:19–20

Question:

Did Noah have to search for all the animals or did they come by themselves? How did they know they had to come to the ark?

Cheyenne

Age 11 — Pennsylvania, USA

Answer:

...two of every kind will come to you to keep them alive (Genesis 6:20)

Cheyenne, the simple answer according to our Bible verse is no, Noah did not have to search the world for the animals because God commanded them to come to the ark. But I would like to explain a bit further so we can see how great our Creator God really is. There are several instances in the Bible where God uses animals to do His bidding. Like when God sent the big fish to swallow Jonah, who did not want to obey. And what about God commanding the ravens to feed Elijah after God sent him out to the wilderness? You see, God is the Creator; He is powerful, mighty, and great. And He clearly chose which animals would join Noah and then He commanded them to go ... and they obeyed. After all, God is the Creator, and they had to obey their Creator (as we need to obey the Creator — the Lord Jesus).

Genesis 6:20, 7:8–9

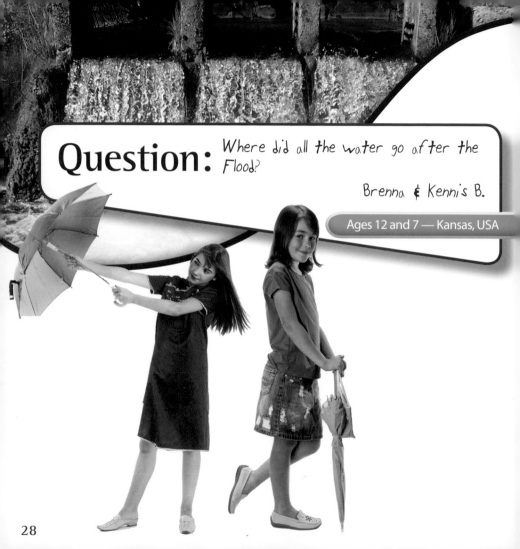

Question: Where did all the water go after the Flood?

Brenna & Kennis B.

Ages 12 and 7 — Kansas, USA

Answer:

The mountains rose, the valleys sank down to the place that you appointed for them (Psalm 104:8 ESV).

Did you know that if the mountains and oceans were leveled off there would be enough water on the earth right now to cover it to a depth of about two miles? Some Bible scholars believe that our Bible verse here describes how God ended the Flood. The mountains rose up and the Flood waters went down where the ocean basins formed. Even evolutionists talk about the mountains being raised up like this, but they believe it happened over a long, long time. We believe that God did it very quickly at the end of the Flood. (By the way, that's why we find so many sea fossils near the top of mountains. Makes sense, doesn't it?) So, where is the water? I believe it is all still here. Did you realize that three-fourths of the earth is still covered with water?! The next time you go to the beach and watch God's powerful ocean, remember you're looking at the waters that once covered the entire earth during the time of the Flood!

Genesis 8:21, 9:11; 2 Peter 2:5

Question: Why aren't there fossils of humans from Noah's flood?

Bailey B.

Age 7 — California, USA

Answer:

So the LORD said, "I will destroy man whom I have created from the face of the earth, both man and beast, creeping thing and birds of the air, for I am sorry that I have made them" (Genesis 6:7).

Most people don't realize there are actually very few fossils of vertebrates (animals that have backbones). Almost all of the fossils ever found have been marine organisms, snails, corals, plants, and insects. In order to become a fossil, a plant or animal needs to be quickly and completely buried. It seems that humans caught in this terrible Flood would try to save themselves any way possible. It is probable that as the Flood rose, humans continued to seek higher ground. As the humans and animals died, many would float and eventually sink — only to be washed away at the end of the Flood, when the mountains rose and the waters rushed off of the earth. Also, there were only two humans to start with — but lots of different animal kinds. So one would expect to find a lot more animal fossils than humans. However, there may be some human fossils somewhere in the world — after all, scientists have dug up very little of the fossil record.

Matthew 24:39; Psalm 29:10

31

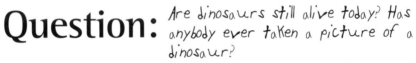

Question: Are dinosaurs still alive today? Has anybody ever taken a picture of a dinosaur?

Sawyer P.

Age 7— South Carolina, USA

Answer:

Look now at the behemoth, which I made along with you...
(Job 40:15–18).

Well, Sawyer, I haven't seen a photograph of a live dinosaur. (It would be cool, though!) But we have something even better than a photo. We have a description from God, our infinite Creator. In our Bible verse God describes a very large, unique animal — one that evidently was living with Job. Now Job didn't have a camera, he couldn't take a photo, so God made sure we'd know just what one of these amazing animals (the dinosaur) looked like. And there's another thing. We do have something called petroglyphs. These are drawings that people carved long ago on rocks. Some of these petroglyphs look a lot like dinosaurs. You know, I believe it is very possible that there may still be dinosaurs in the world, but most of them have probably died out. Maybe there are some in a remote jungle somewhere, just not seen by people. It wouldn't surprise me at all (remember, the average size of a dinosaur was only that of a sheep — and some were as small as chickens), but it would sure surprise evolutionists who say that dinosaurs died out "millions" of years ago.

Isaiah 14:29; Job 41:1, 13–21

33

Question:

Did a meteor really kill all the dinosaurs? Where did all the dinosaurs go?

Abby G.

Age 6 — New Mexico, USA

34

Answer:

Bring out with you every living thing of all flesh that is with you: birds and cattle and every creeping thing that creeps on the earth, so that they may abound on the earth, and be fruitful and multiply on the earth (Genesis 8:17).

The meteor story first started about 1980. Some scientists teach that a huge meteor hit the earth some 65 million years ago and killed all the dinosaurs. Wow! That would be something to see! But I don't believe it happened that way at all. First of all, we know from the Bible that the earth is only about 6,000 years old. Second, why would a meteor strike kill the dinosaurs and leave other animals alive?

So, what did happen to the dinosaurs? Well, Abby, I'll tell you . . . they died! After the Flood, and to this very day, there are many animals that have become extinct (died out) or are on the endangered species list (close to dying out) because of the effects of sin on the earth. Animals become extinct because they are hunted, their land is destroyed, they kill each other, their food supply runs out, or they get diseases that kill them. That is probably exactly what happened to the dinosaurs. It's simple . . . they died!

Genesis 10:9, 8:19

DINO CLUB
HUMANS
ALLOWED

Question: Were there people alive when the dinosaurs roamed the earth?

Jim S.

Age 6 — Georgia, USA

36

Answer:

And God made the beast of the earth according to its kind . . . And God saw that it was good. Then God said, "Let Us make man in Our image, according to Our likeness," . . . Then God saw everything that He had made, and indeed it was very good. So the evening and the morning were the sixth day (Genesis 1:25, 26, 31).

Dinosaurs and people living together? That is really hard to imagine, isn't it, Jim? Actually, it is not hard to imagine if we are Christians who believe God's Word. Look at our Bible verses. God's Word tells us that dinosaurs (beasts of the earth) and man (Adam and Eve) were actually made on the very same 24-hour day. They were all created on Day 6 of Creation Week. And, it is true that dinosaurs are older than people — but by only a few hours, not millions of years! So, what is the answer to your question? Yes! Dinosaurs lived with people — before the Flood, on Noah's ark with Noah and his family, and after the Flood. God's Word also *describes* what I believe was a dinosaur. In the book of Job, the animal called Behemoth is described, and it sure seems to be a unique, dinosaur-like animal (like a large Sauropod), living right there with Job and the people of that time!

Job 40–41

37

Question: Are dinosaurs related to birds?

Kimberly W.

Age 7 — Georgia, USA

38

Answer:

Then God said, ". . . let birds fly above the earth across the face of the firmament of the heavens." . . . So the evening and the morning were the fifth day (Genesis 1:20, 23).

There are many scientists who believe that dinosaurs evolved into birds. But, if we look at God's Word to find the truth, we'll see that this could not be possible. Why? Because the birds, the flying creatures, were created on Day 5. As you have learned, the dinosaurs were made on Day 6. So, actually, dinosaurs were created *after* birds and could never have turned into birds! Another thing, Kimberly, if you look at a bird and consider a dinosaur, you will see that they are totally different kinds of animals. They have different systems of breathing, they have completely different blood systems, and they have very different bone structures. There are just too many differences between the two. They are unique wonderful creatures created by God. Birds are birds and dinosaurs are dinosaurs and that's it!

Genesis 1:22, 1:28; Romans 1:22–23

Question: How could Noah's children fill the earth?

Josh L.

Age 12 — Pennsylvania, US.

40

Answer:

So God blessed Noah and his sons, and said to them: "Be fruitful and multiply, and fill the earth" (Genesis 9:1).

First of all, there are now well over six billion people in the world! I'd say Noah's descendants did a great job of filling the earth. According to the Bible, the Flood was about 4,300 years ago. So, can we account for six billion people starting with only eight just 4,300 years ago? Here is an example for you: Say you get $1.00 on your first birthday. Your parents say they will double your gift on each birthday until you are 21. When you're two you'll get $2, when you're three, you'll get $4, when you're four, you'll get $8, and so on. You just double your birthday gift from the previous year. Well, when you are 21, your gift would be over $1,000,000! Population growth is similar to that. Given enough generations, the number of people being added with each generation would be huge! Just like each of your birthdays above started with more money, each new generation starts with a lot more people. When you do the calculations, you will find that it is very easy to account for six billion people starting with only eight after the Flood.

Genesis 1:28, 9:7

Question:

The books we get from the library state that caves and cave formations took thousands of years to form. We wondered how long they really took and if or how they were related to the world-wide flood.

Adrian & Isaiah W.

Age 10 and 6 — Pennsylvania, US

42

Answer:

They had to live in the clefts of the valleys,
In caves of the earth and the rocks (Job 30:6).

We find cave systems all over our country and the world. I believe most of these cave systems were formed over a short amount of time, not over thousands or millions of years. When we start with the Bible, we see that Noah's flood created conditions that were just perfect for forming all kinds of intricate caves. The water covering the earth left thick layers of limestone and other layers. When the Flood ended, the mountains rose, the valleys sank, and the water flowed off the earth's surface and seeped through the soft sediments. Because water can contain acid dissolved from the air and the soil, this would eat away at the limestone, forming caves. There are also other ways caves can be formed quickly. The dramatic events associated with the flood of Noah's day provided excellent conditions for quick cave formation.

Genesis 8:3, 19:30; 1 Kings 18:13; John 11:38

Question:
Why doesn't the Bible tell us about the Ice Age?

Jemima F.

Age 10 — Northern Ireland

44

Answer:

... on that day all the fountains of the great deep were broken up, and the windows of heaven were opened (Genesis 7:11).

The Bible is a book of history and altogether true, but God does not reveal everything to us in this book. However, if we look at what we know about the worldwide flood from the Bible, then look at the evidence of glaciers and ice sheets that once covered at least one-third of the earth, we see that the Bible does give us some clues about the Ice Age. A catastrophe as huge as Noah's flood drastically changed the climate on the earth, creating conditions perfect for an Ice Age at the end of the Flood.

The Bible tells us that the fountains of the great deep burst forth. This was unlike anything that we can even imagine! This breaking up of the earth caused the oceans to heat up and caused ash and dust to fill the air, blocking out sunlight, making the temperatures on earth cooler. As the warm water from the oceans evaporated into the air, forming clouds, the colder air over the earth caused wintry conditions, lots of snow, and ice glaciers. This could have very easily caused an Ice Age that lasted hundreds of years. When we start with what the Bible tells us, we can find the truth!

Look at our verse in Job. Maybe this is a reference to the Ice Age at the time of Job.

Job 37:9–10

45

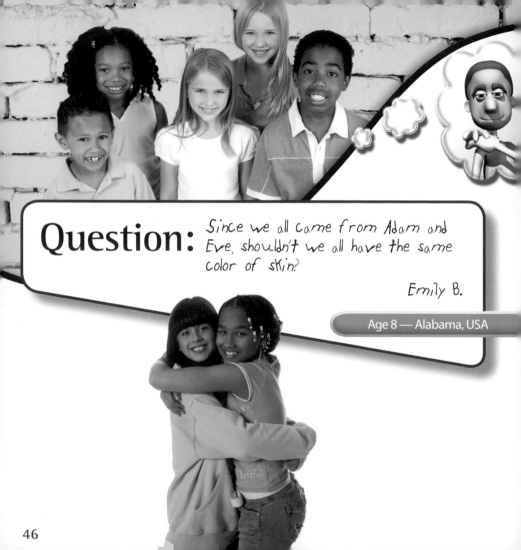

Question: Since we all came from Adam and Eve, shouldn't we all have the same color of skin?

Emily B.

Age 8 — Alabama, USA

46

Answer:

And He has made from one blood every nation of men to dwell on all the face of the earth, and has determined their preappointed times and the boundaries of their dwellings (Acts 17:26).

For the answer to this question, you'll need a mirror and a white or black piece of paper. Now, if you consider yourself a white, light-colored person, look in the mirror and hold the white piece of paper next to your face. You aren't white at all, are you? If you are a dark-skinned, "black" person, get the black piece of paper, hold it next to your face, and look in the mirror. Are you really black? No! People are some shade of brown, because we all have a brown pigment in our skin called melanin. This is what makes us the shade of color that we are. Some people have a lot of melanin and they would be very dark; some people don't have as much melanin, they would be lighter. I think that Adam and Eve had a medium brown amount of pigment. From such two medium brown people, they would be able to pass on the genes to either produce a really dark child or a really light child. So, Emily, to answer your question, we all do have the same type of skin color . . . it is just that the amount of melanin (brown color) differs from person to person.

Genesis 9:19, 11:9

47

Answers Are Always Important!

The Answers Book for Kids answers questions from children around the world in this four-volume series. Each volume will answer 22 questions in a friendly and readable style appropriate for children 6–12 years old; and each covers a unique topic including, *Creation and the Fall; Dinosaurs and the Flood of Noah; God and the Bible;* and *Sin, Salvation, and the Christian Life.* Explore:

- Why the first person God created was a boy.
- How Adam named all the animals.
- Why the Bible is true.
- What being "born again" means.

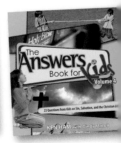